Table of Contents

Bears!

Look in the tree!
Hello, bear!

Body Parts

Bears have
thick fur.
Most bears are
black or brown.

fur

Bears have
sharp claws.
They dig
and climb.

claws

Bears have big noses. They can smell food!

This **cub**
takes food
left by people.
Uh-oh!

cub

Bears do not eat in winter. They sleep in **dens**.

den

Spring is here
at last!
Wake up, bear!

Bear Facts

Bear Body Parts

fur

nose

claws

Bear Food

fruit

grass

fish

Glossary

cub

a baby bear

dens

homes built
by animals

prey

animals that
are hunted

To Learn More

ON THE WEB

FACTSURFER

Factsurfer.com gives you a safe, fun way to find more information.

1. Go to www.factsurfer.com.

2. Enter "bears" into the search box and click 🔍.

3. Select your book cover to see a list of related content.

Index

The images in this book are reproduced through the courtesy of: fluidmediafactory, front cover; Daria Rybakova, p. 3; Paul Winterman, p. 5; Volodymyr Burdiak, p. 7; Vishnevskiy Vasily, p. 8; Christina Radcliffe, p. 9; Gagat55, p. 11; giedre vaitekune, p. 12; Jerry Sharp, p. 13 (top); Allen Paul Photography, p. 13 (bottom left); CSNafzger, p. 13 (bottom right); alexmgn, p. 15; Eyal Nahmias/ Alamy, p. 17; Andreas Argirakis, pp. 18, 23 (dens); Nature Picture Library/ ALamy, p. 19; Maryna Shkvyria, p. 21; notsuperstar, p. 22 (top); BGSmith, p. 22 (fruit); 1827photo, p. 22 (grass); Sekar B, p. 22 (fish); Kelly vanDellen, p. 23 (cub); karamysh, p. 23 (prey).